The WEIGHT of SNOW

NEW & SELECTED POEMS

B. L. BRUCE

BLACK SWIFT PRESS

Copyright © 2014 by B. L. Bruce

All rights reserved. First printed in 2014.

ISBN-13 (eBook): 978-0-9914503-0-5
ISBN-13 (trade paperback): 978-0-9914503-1-2

In accordance with the U.S. Copyright Act of 1976, the scanning, uploading, and electronic sharing of any part of this book without permission of the publisher constitute unlawful piracy and theft of the author's intellectual property. No part of this book may be reproduced or transmitted in any form or by any means, electronic or mechanical, including photocopying, recording, or by any information storage and retrieval system, except for excerpts used for reviews, without permission in writing from the publisher.

Cover design by Bri Bruce and Kermit Heartsong
Cover image courtesy Shutterstock, Inc.

Published by Black Swift Press, an imprint of B.B. Productions

Visit www.bribruceproductions.squarespace.com for more information.

A special thanks to those involved in the publication of this work. It would not have been possible without your encouragement and support.

Some poems first appeared in the following publications: *Tattoo Highway*, *Red Fez Entertainment*, *Northwind Magazine*, *The Avocet Review*, *The Cossack*, *phren-Z*, *The Soundings Review*, *Third Wednesday*, *The Wayfarer*, *The Monterey Poetry Review*, and *2River View*.

PRAISE FOR *The Weight of Snow*

The poems in The Weight of Snow *are heartfelt, skillfully written, and keenly observed fragments of the natural world and our lives there. Bravo.*

- Gary Young, Poet Laureate of Santa Cruz County, Award-Winning Author of *No Other Life, Braver Deeds*, and *Pleasure*

The Weight of Snow *belongs on your bookshelf or coffee table. Keep it close by. The beautiful cover and title itself evoke soul—and then what a treat to open the pages! The poetry is a subtle example of the paradox of soul; for example, it captures both innocence and disillusionment. It is haunting and provocative while simple and natural. The author's amazing gift of poetic writing and presentation cannot be missed—it's on every page. Very touching. The poems have that rare quality of taking on new meaning with every read. It is so much more than a book of poems—but you must experience it yourself. This is a book to have and to hold--and then make sure to send one to a friend.*

- Dr. Linda R. Harper, Author of *Eat: A Guide to Discovering Your Natural Relationship with Food* and *The Power of Joy in Giving to Animals*

The best poems are evocative, powerful and transporting. They take you to places, memories, situations or allow you to live vicariously through the experiences of another. The Weight of Snow *is such a book from beginning to end. It is not a collection of disjointed poems, thrown together. It is a poignant and beautiful story of a life, experiences, memories and pain. Ms. Bruce is truly a gifted poet and one need only read the first poem, to understand her talent and what this book holds. I highly recommend* The Weight of Snow *for how it touches, reveals, informs and for its beautiful simplicity.*

- K. E. Heartsong, Publisher at Taylen Lane Publishing and Author of *Illusions, Dystopia & Monsters: How the Truths of Our Time May Be Stranger Than Fiction*

The Weight of Snow *is alive with style and filled with beautiful, nostalgic imagery. Bruce's free verse poetry is rich with detail, and her evocative language will stay with you long after reading this collection. Deeply introspective and profoundly insightful, each new poem displays great thematic range and literary sensibility. I have no doubt that Bruce will be a strong and important voice for modern poetry. I look forward to her future publications!*

- J. Rodriguez, Film Producer and Artist

By her descriptive portrayal of the natural world, Bruce would make Mother Nature herself blush with pride. One can expect to find deep meaning and a sense of soulfulness in her poetic language. The poems reflect a passion and desire to know and grasp life with reverence. They stand as testimony to the necessary guardianship that we all must be responsible for in preserving our world and knowing our place in it.

- D. J. White, Wildlife Biologist

[Bruce] has an amazing ability to bring tremendous depth to the most simple of life's treasures and experiences. With thoughtful

insights of a perceptive, educated writer, Bri Bruce eliminates the line between the importance of humankind and nature, and combines them in an exquisite presentation of literary brilliance, leaving the reader looking for answers to questions they never even knew they had.

- Heidi Lewin, Life Coach and Counselor

B. L. Bruce's recent work features keenly observed human interactions with nature. She uses spare but effective descriptions to illuminate the natural world and our response to it. Her sharp perceptions about human wildlife ("The Blue Scarf") also resonated with me. Love, loss, and the eternal solace of nature. She is the worthy heiress of Mary Oliver.

- John Gilchrist

Contents

Eggs for Dumplings 1

Crossing Alma Bridge 3

Fly Fishing the High Sierras 5

Desert Moon 7

Crossing the Meadow 9

Clay 11

Westlake Pond 13

What Remains 15

Endings 17

Navarro River 19

Indian Summer 21

Memory 23

November in Half Moon Bay 25

Narrowed 27

Pleasures 29

Ghost 31

Drought	33
What I Am Not	35
Sand Dollar Beach	37
Rainsong	39
Between the Hours	41
Fragility	43
The Weight of Snow	45
Out of Solitude	47
Migration	49
Monsoon	51
Shearwaters	53
South of Davenport	55
The Blue Scarf	57
The Button	59
Saplings	61
I Remember	63
Hailstorm	65
The Sparrow	67
The Sea	69

At Henry Cowell State Park, Early
Winter.. 71
Snow.. 73
Morning...................................... 75
The Summit Fires 77
Climbing North Mountain in Spring .. 79
The Butterfly Tree......................... 81
We Listen.................................... 83
To Watch the Angry Sea................ 85
Traveling East............................. 87
Infinite....................................... 89
The Leaving 91
January Morning 93
Two Figures on a Train 95
The Unlearning of Fear 97
Lake Audrian, Midwinter................ 99

The WEIGHT of SNOW

Eggs for Dumplings

In the dark kitchen, you crack
eggs for dumplings, drunk with
the ebbing heat of summer
and berry wine. As I look on,
I can see you there in dim light
falling to pieces.

We walk into the garden,
watch throngs of honeybees
nose up to the lavender and sip.
The dog's body now buried
in the hot earth, the sorrows
of your heart knowing the sighs
of the doves. In the trees, the jays
greet the dusk, blue as bruises.

We stand barefoot
beside the crooked oak
and throw pebbles into the twilight sky.
Heads thrown back, we watch bats
dive in their silent pursuit, unknowing.

Crossing Alma Bridge

I see that spring has faded
from the dogwood trees.
Hemlock and foxglove bend
to meet the earth in the heat,
beginning again from seed.

You draw closer not because
I call to you, but in the smell of
freesia, the taste of salt.
I think about loving you:
frightened child in a thunderstorm.

Below, the swift creek meanders
around the manzanita. Swallows
nesting beneath the bridge take
to the air, dip at the surface
of the narrow stream,
stilling their wings
to glide so effortlessly
beyond the bend.

Fly Fishing the High Sierras

No more can I imagine
the impossible stillness
of the lake at dawn,
than I can see the arc of your line
above the water.

You work a fly along the shores
stepping between granite boulders,
the high Sierra frost of dawn
in your bones.

Almost, I can hear the whir of your leader,
the tick of your reel,
a fin work at the water's surface.
Later, you will sit warming by a fire
stoked by fallen pine,
the hiss of sap a symphony at dusk.

Tonight you will dream
of the fish you've pulled up
from the green depths, wrestled ashore,
and in the tenfold silence that follows,
glimpse the clarity of the stars
in the seamless night.

Desert Moon

Gibbous moon over Sea of Cortez,
now black in the night.
I wake to sounds of whales surfacing
in the calm bay, stirred
from dreams of catching a Dorado,
only to watch the dimming
of the impossible colors: indigo,
mustard, viridian, crimson.

And I, haunted by my selfish guilt,
wishing to undo it
and give the fish back to the sea,
ask to what end do we betray the earth
if not through the armistice of death?
What of this difference
between lion and lamb?
We are not saints,
these last wild places
disappearing.

Desert wind twists through the dry *arroyo*
and pires of *cordon,* dust-green saguaro cactus.
A gull, yet to roost, weeps from the sand.

Crossing The Meadow

May dawn coming,
a thin rain falls. I tread a path
through low marsh grass
wondering if you have forgotten
our nakedness, frantic like children
      in the cold,
sun rising beyond the dark woods,
dreams that twist nearer,
the splitting apart of our souls.

I listen to a lark chirrup in the reeds
beside a bay laurel,
flitting—hurried and winded—
above the meadow,
trampled and slick with dew
where the mule deer have bedded down
in the night.

Without dreams,
you feel heat in place of love,
      sun on stone,
      skin on skin.
Along the far edge of the meadow, I stop
only to think of leaving you.
A jay calls into the stillness of the trees,

a branch snaps from a tall fir,
falling to the ground.
I turn, and walk
into the woods.

CLAY

I come knocking, find you in the garden
looking not more than a child, eating
the sweet petals of the guava blossoms,
bending to sweep the stone pathway.

You drift impatiently into the house,
in one room, then out, the easiness
of your movements unbothered by age
in the sweet, unfurling air of spring.

Sweat beginning to bead at the backs
of my knees, I know your face
just as you do in the mirror, see we are
fashioned from the same clay.

You understand the restlessness in me,
eyes carrying that burden of knowing,
like the towhee on the sill staring at its own
reflection, that desperate sound of wing-beat
against glass, wanting so much to be nearer.

Westlake Pond

Water falling from clouds:
low footbridge over a pair of swans
in the bulrushes, slender necks
bending to dance. Rain beads
along white feathers, gathers
and slips into the dark water.
Even the robin sings through the storm.

From the corner of my eye,
a shadow moves. When I look
I see it is only the wind swaying the willows
at the pond's edge.

The air grows colder,
and I think of you.

What Remains

What remains weeks after you've left:
droplets of dew on the window
from your bath, since evaporated,
now gray circles—ghosts,
wounds still to heal.

Think of our final days,
your hands—those that taught me to hate—
the large rock at the north end of the beach,
the place beside it where you told me to undress
and lie down on the sand, skin puckering
in the cold.

Only in your absence
can I unfold in quiet places,
put ice in my wine without remorse,
honey-haired and wild-eyed.

Endings

In the waning darkness,
the southern valley wide,
mountains violet with distance:
white snowfields cut between low fences
and rows of poplars, their leaves
now shaken away.

I think only of spring, tiring of the way
winter erases everything, covers all with
the wisdom of endings—
the songs of the river silenced,
snow-veiled trees unmoving—
the heaviness of nothing.

From behind the thin curtains
at the window, I hear the pines breaking.

NAVARRO RIVER

Once again, the wide river browns with silt,
rising. The kingfisher has noisily gone to roost
along the east bank. An egret crouches in the reeds.

To the west, curving steeply beyond dying willows
worn from the footwork of cormorants,
steam rises, then dissipates
into the Pacific sky.

Indian Summer

The cherry trees are blooming late,
the flame of the Chinese pistache
clinging to thinning limbs,
autumn days starved of cold.

For hours, I sit idly beneath the maple
reading, then pause to watch sparrows
scratch at the ground, their shadows
sliding over leaves—so much
like hands on skin.

Beside the dusty path, sunflowers turn
their faces toward the midday sky,
acacia trees in full yellow bloom.
The milkweed butterflies begin to cluster
beneath the eaves of the barn.

I rise to pluck a branch of cherry blossoms,
hold it to my nose wishing there were
more ways to stay what moments
we no longer keep.

Memory

Now etched like a scar, a language
I cannot understand, I lean
by the window, sunlight on my back.
A sparrow signals morning,
Junegrass blooms silently.

Recalling wind between granite boulders,
over fallen white pine, young hemlock,
Genoa City busied far below—
I still do not envy it. Before sunlight
reached the western mountain ridge,
I kept the company of the dark valley,
the waking of the world from sleep,
voices of unfamiliar birds.

Early skies were cloudless, the moon still
hanging in the north untroubled by daylight,
and suddenly I could not remember your face,
the youth surely having left it—
the deaths of our elders
the only signal of time.

We spent long nights drinking wine
and learning the histories of our family,
playing dominoes by candlelight—
now and again I hear the sound of them
on the wooden table.

This morning, winter ends and color
returns to the garden, meadows
stirred by movements other than wind.

November in Half Moon Bay

Heavy mist beyond Pillar Point—
how many times waves beat upon the coast,
then withdrew?
I feel only that stumbling of my heart
at the sight of the sea—
the nakedness of the Pacific in winter,
the pensive moods of the gulls—
and it is this tumult
beside the sea that haunts,
salt in my veins.

Narrowed

In four short years, there is much
we don't remember. Having studied
a calendar, an entire year before me,
the grouping of days seem not at all
to amount to their title. I had soon learned
how the body, unmarred by time,
moves in the light of gray morning.
Now, we grow thicker, more unsure,
our shapes changing. In the quickening
of days, I leave notes for you while you're out,
poems at your bedside. I knead bread
while you sleep in the other room, listen
for your stirring, wait for your return.
Even when alone, I stay narrowed to
one side of the bed.

Pleasures

More autumn months graced by frost,
the flowering quince dies. I set out
to walk the edge of the woods,
think of all the pleasures in being alone.
Beyond the wide reach of the old oak,
I rest.

Soon, I see the kestrel
devouring a sparrow,
then fly west toward the sea.

Ghost

In the middle of the afternoon,
she lays out her dead lover's clothes:
green plaid jacket, white t-shirt,
blue denim jeans. A pair of sneakers
rests side by side, one sole agape
at the toe. She watches the clothes
as if they might come alive,
flesh filling the hollows of the soft fabric
the way wind pushes a ship under sail.
Folded into a chair on the far end of the room,
she smokes a cigarette in her underwear,
while the clothing lies vacant, expectant.

Drought

In the still air, heavied beneath
a half-moon, clusters of seedlings uproot
on the path through the garden.

I spend the night reading by firelight,
book of poems propped open, wine-stained
and dog-eared, wishing I had sooner discovered
the words of the ancients. Everywhere seeming
to turn to dust, the unfailing green of old worlds
barely a memory, I tire of one book,
pick up another — bottle of wine soon emptied
on the bookcase.

Outside, the mercy of the drought—
unbearable heat even in darkness.
My mother paces in the kitchen,
the well gone dry. We dream
of water dripping from the wisteria.

What I Am Not

This morning, rising,
I stop to stare at my own naked body,
breasts like two dark eyes, accusing,
then quickly dress.

Sometimes feeling like no more
than a corpse, I beg:
*Look, see what
you've done to me.*

I am not the same as I was
as if, in these endless dying days,
there occurs nothing but a building
of what I am not:
something skittish—
the gray fox at dawn.

Sand Dollar Beach

In a thick curtain of fog,
the tide ebbs and falls away;
oyster shells, a broken sand dollar
fleck the stretch of dark sand.

I am taken by surprise
when a fisherman emerges from the mist.
He is silent, nods beneath a straw hat;
after casting his line into the surf,
he stabs his fishing pole into the sand,
lays a net at his feet, crosses his arms
over his chest. His face is furrowed, solemn,
weathered by sun and wind—the marks
of years spent beside the sea.

A godwit wades at the edge of the surf
eyeing me from the spray;
sanderlings alight in the sand, stand
at my advance—one takes to the air,
drifts south over the bay.

Rainsong

What of this winter here?
The unhappy song of rain and
wind in the bay laurel,
rainwater in the fountain
a mixing of what is ours
and what is not.

I go to the meadow
when the storm has slowed
to see what has changed,
what unknowable thirst was quenched:
the howl and fury in the night
brought down the tall sequoia
and with it one hundred years,
the osprey's nest, my childhood.

Between the Hours

The clock ticks on the bedside table.
At a shifting of weight, I whisper
your name in the dark, then see
the moon among the blinds,
find solace. In misery, I have
prayed for strength. In faith,
we find faults. We know only
the faces of others, not their hearts,
unbearable loneliness the ember
in love's wake. In the cleft between
the hours, I wait for daylight.

Fragility

From my mother
I learned how wine swims in the vein,
what happens when the vaquita dies,
how to boil meat from bone
to make chicken soup.
Like her, often I am stirred from sleep
by thought, not dream.

A frenzied rap at the thin door a beckon
to follow her into the summer garden,
we listen to the birds—
nighthawk in the oak,
mockingbird in the underbrush.
We busy ourselves wondering what dark place
becomes the bed of the crow.

In these moments, we are suddenly aware
that our hearts are beating—there is
something larger than ourselves.

And knowing the fragility of it all,
we speak the language of mortality.

The Weight of Snow

Waking one morning in late November,
lured by the crimson in the elms,
I watch a busied thrush push his wings
through the autumn leaves.
He hurries from branch to branch,
then finally settles, though nervous
and wide-eyed, as it rains.

In their sudden bareness
after a quiet autumn,
I expect the elm's limbs
will bend under the weight of snow
as they did in the grip of the thrush.

    At the first sign of winter,
I will greet the snow that falls mutely
beyond the fogged windows of the small kitchen,
remembering how we danced one morning—
across marbled tiles in the watchful eye
of the cold winter sun.

    But now,
the red elms in the yard
and the cluster of berries on the Toyon bush
shiver in the dawn.

Leaves fall from the alders in wind.
I've grown older. When I look again
for the small wood thrush, he is gone,
somehow, without me noticing.

Out of Solitude

I hear laughter beyond the fence
suddenly feeling unalone in the sounds
of others living: traffic on the highway,
coughing in the other room. Uneasy
waxwings screech in the pyracantha,
and through the paned window
I watch twilight arrive like greeting
an old friend. How strange to journey
out of weeks of solitude and discover
our humanness, that presence
of others.

MIGRATION

Shipyard in late spring heat,
harbor docks in the steady heave of tide—
waves push upon the shoreline,
draw back. I had seen
some years ago
a migration of thousands—
small cetaceans, *Tursiops truncates*,
dance at the bow of a passing ship.

Now, in the distance,
the sea widens.
finned passage north—
blue fluke on gray horizon.
Farther across the Pacific,
a cove in Taiji:
blood in the swelling
of tide.

Monsoon

In the wet season, the women gather
in a clearing among tall stalks of papaya,
waxy banana leaves. In the shelter
of a mango tree, they undress, unwrap the cloths
swaddling their bodies, and laugh. Naked, they dance
in circles. A torrent of rain falls, slips
over their breasts as it is pulled to the humid earth—
against their hips, along the lengths of bare leg.
Puddling in the ground at their feet, rainwater
gathers in small pools, held delicately inside
their footprints in the black mud.

Shearwaters

A red barn rises broad-shouldered
beyond rows of eggplant, heirloom tomatoes,
red cabbage. Migrant workers bend
into the low fields in mimic of the leaning cypress—
pushed by eastward winds
in its years rooted beside the sea.

A man in a straw hat pauses
over a neat file of butter lettuce,
squints into the short California dusk.
A blue heron flies east.
Black shearwaters arrive
from the south.

South of Davenport

A gull rolling in the surf,
one gray, twisted wing
fallen limp—I shepherd the bird
against oncoming waves;
he settles, gives in to me.

When I see there is nothing I can do—
bright stain of blood on white feathers—
I set him down at the foot of a sandstone cliff.
He does not struggle, but rises slowly instead,
toddles back to the sea.

Later, bending to wash the blood
from my hands, I think
there is something to be said
about the way an animal dies.

Days later, I help a woman
pluck a battered loon from a tangle of kelp,
cradle it in her jacket.
In her arms, the loon sang, weary-eyed,
leaving behind the anguish of wavework,
of being washed upon the shore with the
driftwood, the trash,
the used needles,
wings outspread on wet sand.

The Blue Scarf

Tuesday morning—rain. A woman
holds the Sunday paper above her head,
slips beneath a low awning along
Pacific Avenue. Unwrapping a blue scarf
from her neck, I see her nylons are ripped.
Hair dripping, she pulls at the hem
of her skirt, adjusts the collar of her coat.
Her eyes meet mine. Her black mascara
runs, and I cannot tell what is rain
and what are tears.

The Button

You had pulled at my sweater
in the night. It wasn't until morning
that I saw the button missing
after leaving you dreaming,
having walked to town, my shirtfront agape—
a mouth knowing the wet of your tongue.

Years later, I find the button
in the pocket of an old shirt, suddenly recalling
I had tucked it away, eyes blurred with wine,
and blamed you.

The sweater, now gone, perhaps worn
undone by another, I have forgotten your face,
that carefulness in your voice now of no importance to
me—so quickly we can love, as quickly the heart
becomes impervious.

Saplings

I had not gone walking
beneath the trees since last spring.
When the redwoods fell
at the cutting of the saws, I felt it—
the echo in the canyon,
carrying with it a century.

This evening, as the skies darkened,
I saw from the jagged stumps
new spears of saplings rising,
reaching to meet sky.

I Remember

I remember my great grandmother,
spreading her ashes
in Sycamore Valley wind,
watching as the gray dust settled.

Squinting in the bright heat,
we are quiet, my father tacit
and enduring beside me,
yet seeming bemused, his brow furrows
like a child wondering where we go
when we die—a blackness
beyond our last moments
like that which we are born from.

And again, when older,
looking to the black sky,
standing in the open, searching foolishly
beneath Pleiades and Cassiopeia
pleading, *What more?*

I saw that the ash was not carried off,
but hung instead
in the summer marsh grass,
on the tall stalks of reeds
along the edges of a small frog pond,
surface glittered as if a heavy snow
had fallen and lay unmelted.

I was a child then,
cradling an urn in the crook of my arm,
Devil Mountain breaking the east horizon.
I knew about death.

Hailstorm

A hailstorm interrupts the still morning,
pit-patting on ground hardened with frost.
Among other sights, the sky darkens,
high clouds over black mountains,
the sea a pale gray roughed by wind.
The brown hens settle in their boxes.
The thick leaves of the magnolia blanket the lawn.

The wet sheen of rain and sleet on your neck,
you wander through rows of apple trees,
nearly bare. My eyes trace the lines
etched on your face. The chill a sudden
flood to my bones, I reach for you—
palm to palm, your heat like the sweet bite
of a ripe fuyu in autumn.

When the hail stops, you pause,
tilting your head backward upon that same
rain-wet neck and I see tomorrow, see poetry
in the angle of your throat, then the ocean in your
eyes, its tides pulsing in my veins.

The Sparrow

As the wild grasses begin to die,
a raven calls from the distant oaks.
A vulture's shadow moves
across the hills. I pace the garden,
finding a young sparrow
floating in the birdbath.

For a moment, I hold the still body
as if to test its heft in my palm,
the lightness of life.

I settle for burying
what remains of the sparrow,
who, when living, would flit
ever warily among the thin limbs
of the crepe myrtle—
I remind myself
God has created,
just as He can destroy,
and move to grab the hand shovel,
digging a hole beside
the Black-eyed Susans.

The Sea

Never has the cold crept into my bones
in quite this way—a chill as if I have
shaken off heavy clothes and gone
running naked into the water,
later feeling it seep from me,
north sea in my blood.

Dark muse of winter, my mercurial
lover: chorus of rain, reeds colliding in wind;
the pounding of surf like hearing your own heart
beat in your ears.

Lightning flickers over the Santa Lucia Mountains.
Stretching past the tideline,
the swollen moon dances in the dark bay—
I think of Li Po on the bank of the Yangtze River.
Perhaps he, too, saw a woman lying bare,
shivering in the cold.

At Henry Cowell State Park, Early Winter

In fall,
the big leaf maples warm
    in color,
and in time will let go
their dying leaves.
By December, the ungiving stalks
of the American Sweetgum are bare
      and still,
          even in wind.

We walk beside the woodyard
late one afternoon,
and my mother says,
    The leaves are turning
    on the alders,
        and nods.

Her skin, the best clock,
    a sundial in the angled light;
I do not know her younger years,
or the likeness of her gait at my age,
but I can recognize crow's feet
at the edge of her eyes,
the furrowed hands
    that have bathed me,
        cradled me.

I drop a glove in a puddle of rainwater,
        and bending to remove it
see the reflection of my mother's figure,
see the levy of years—
the unexpected wither of skin
        as if waking to see
        that it has snowed
               overnight.

Snow

Glow of moonlight blurring into dawn,
the far mountains dusted in frost,
I pull myself from sleep, dress
in a heavy coat
to spend the morning
wading through snow. I admire
the hushing of the earth,
then listen to the quiet of it falling
from the weighted bows of pines—
downy flakes sink over the small pond,
yet to ice over, water mingling
with what is little more,
then perishing. From the timberline:
the incensed cawing of a nutcracker.
Sooner or later, I know,
we all return to where we came from.
Still, years turn from me.
I consider the meaning of eternity,
our quiet days ever numbered.

Morning

He keeps in memory the way
he half-woke in the night,
hand fumbling in the unfilled space beside him,
then returning to sleep.

When morning advances
through the window,
his breath paints the air.
A feeble hiss from the gas heater,
the wet rasp of sleet against
the windowpanes
stir him, punctuating the air,
heavy with stillness.

Leafless persimmon trees
in the side yard: orange fruit
dripping from each bare bough,
trembling with robins
and young finches,
whose matted feathers
unsettle against the pending snow.
Above, the sky swells
thick with clouds
pushing their shoulders
into the sky.

He brings to mind again
the sharp edge of her jaw,

the soft patter of pulse
in his ears, quickening;
come spring: wild irises in mason
jars on the windowsills;
a hairpin in the crevice
of his floorboards.

And at this,
morning breaks.

The Summit Fires

By the lemon tree
on Melrose Avenue,
I watched a pillar of smoke
crawl into the sky.

In the quiet streets, crowds gathered,
held their breath;
children cried.

When the red lick of flames
surrendered to ash thick as snow
beneath the trees
that burned through the night:
my footprints in a row
like geese flying north.

Climbing North Mountain in Spring

Sonata of the mockingbirds
from the high limbs of the poplar,
the curtains shift;
petals are loosened
from the tangle of bougainvillea vine,
are pulled to the earth
in a brilliant snow of tangerine and magenta.

I go north,
the noise too unsettling,
climb small Sugarloaf Mountain to
wander through redwoods,
the valley hidden in mist.

For now, only the quiet words
of the wind, hum of cicadas;
thoughts of you like mountain streams,
unending.

The Butterfly Tree

In the heat, sweat slips
between her breasts,
pools in the folds
of her belly,
wide and slack
in the taint of
bearing children.
Swallowing two blue pills
in the lamp's glow,
she pulls tight the skin
around her eyes,
thinks of how she fused herself
to another at dawn, empty wineglass
on the bedside table.
Over a distant row of cedars,
the blooming heat of Venus
fixed in lilac sky,
the hot sun rises.
A cricket is stilled
by a wind in the grass.
The butterfly tree shivers.

We Listen

I follow my mother on the narrow
path through the woods, that pure,
undeniable smell of earth and silence
dizzying. The bones of winter trees
clatter together. Birds sing, we listen.
You beam and name them—phoebe, wren,
purple finch—teach me their voices.

The sun falls beyond the trees—I wish
the moment to carry on until the last of my days.
Reminded of my youth, I've missed
the feeling of a day through the eyes
of a child, seeming to totter on endlessly.

With the surrender of evening, we reach
Burns Creek, step out of our shoes to wade
over smooth stones as it begins to rain.

To Watch the Angry Sea

A black-shouldered kite rises quickly, startled
out of the thistle. Beneath a crescent moon
in the dust-colored sky, we watch the anger
of the sea after the storm. Your gaze wanders south,
trips along the shoreline: a pair of oystercatchers
in the out-tide, harem of sea lions in the tangle of
driftwood. I draw nearer, but know I'll never reach
you, not even in dream. In my wanting, I am ugly,
wishing us fused as blood and water. Over the hiss
of waves, the tumult of surf, terns dance above the sea,
the gray gulls laugh.

Traveling East

Unbroken miles of sugar maples
blush in late autumn; in wind,
the poplars stir. Beside a blue farmhouse,
a mule deer missteps over a stream
and settles a path through thick meadow.
Now, before dusk, we drift along a highway
past shadows of birch trees, the pale trunks
fragile and white as bones.

Infinite

A woman in the distance
wades into the ashen sea,
bends to hold it in her hands.
I, too, see that perpetuity—
water blurring into sky—
wanting some small piece
of infinity. Trying to fathom
such boundlessness, I forget
myself standing on the shore,
breathing, living.

The Leaving

By the heavy glass doors,
you kneel to gather scattered clothes,
your naked silhouette a shadow
against the violet dawn.
I know this shape your body makes
against the sky.

A leaf falls from the black oak tree.
I see a flash of rust-red—the robin's breast
before the window. You brush the hair
from your forehead.
Somewhere along the avenue a machine
      is breathing,
and I watch the steady rise and fall
of your bare chest.

I hold myself back, only to reason—
were I a dog curled at your feet,
would you have held me then?
Will you remember me
when you are gone, as I
remember spring
when the first snow falls?

At your passing of the bedside:
your dappled skin, the smell of sea salt.

I turn away from faint rustlings
in the small kitchen,
the quiet unlatch of the door.

January Morning

You hurry through the house, open windows,
leave doors wide open. Sun lights
the confused array of bare branches,
softened earth. A breeze carries warm air
into the kitchen, lifts a few papers from the table.

For a moment, I think I smell summer,
but am quickly reminded otherwise,
the skin on my bare shoulder dimpling.

The dog sleeps by the chair, lazied by sun.
When I run a hand over my tired face,
she lifts her head, old eyes foggy,
but seeing, understanding. How simple
to spend your days dreaming.

Two Figures on a Train

This morning the cattails sway
in the heaviness of red-winged
blackbirds and their sputtering chatter.
Among marsh reeds,
the subtle croaks of toads
echo through glassless windows.

And because neither had imagined
the stillness of the deserted
railway cars bordering the old millpond,
their hands slid beneath soft cotton—
two nude figures startling mice
beneath the floorboards, wetting the dust
on a wooden bench below cobwebs
in the eaves.

They dress and climb down the ladder
away from the train tracks.
The girl steps over oiled ties and scrap steel
ahead of the boy who looks away,
watching the splash of red and yellow
on the black wings of the birds in the reeds.

The Unlearning of Fear

You came through the door
smelling of cold mountain air,
the persimmons in your fist much smaller
after a long autumn without rain.
The rest are left for the birds to pick apart,
you said. The night before last we watched
the opossum climb the slick limbs to eat—
nature has a way of knowing not to waste.

As you bent to greet me,
I found joy in the pace of your heartbeat—
one thousand drums in the stillness of winter.
The fog of your breath
settled between us.

Then, I was made to unlearn fear,
the maw it creates when I am left in silence,
knowing the restless demons brooding in you—
your anger in the dark,
with years, my nervousness,
conversations through closed doors.

Frost thick forming on the roofline,
from the balcony I heard the warblers
screaming in the lemon tree.

Lake Audrian, Midwinter

The prints of a cottontail leading
to a stand of winter aspens, I follow,
plod through new snowfall,
the crystalline sounds of it
meeting midwinter silence
like glass shattering,
salt spilling. I step out
onto the frozen lake,
crouch, and run my fingers along a
crack in the ice. I feel the thunder
of it shifting beneath me as if I were enough
to make the earth move.

www.ingramcontent.com/pod-product-compliance
Lightning Source LLC
Chambersburg PA
CBHW031451040426
42444CB00007B/1058